ROSALYN M. LAMPKIN

THOUGHTS ABOUT LIVING:
FROM *SunRise* TO *SunSet*

Print information available on the last page.

Rev. date: 08/20/2018

To order additional copies of this book, contact:
Xlibris
1-888-795-4274
www.Xlibris.com
Orders@Xlibris.com

ACKNOWLEDGEMENT

I wish to express my sincere gratitude to Mr. Michael Connors, the founder of Morguefile. com as well as Kevin Connors, Johannes Seemann and Emily Beeson.

I also want to thank Morguefile.com all-star team of moderators: Charlie, Kenn, Emily, Stuart and Dawn for maintaining the website to make is very easy and enjoyable to find the perfect photos I used in this book.

SPECIAL THANKS

Photographer(s)	Poem Title
StefaninLA	Cover Image
Jdurham	Book of Secrets
jkt_de	Ship of life
Prawny	Gentle World
Hotblack (2 Photos used)	Gentle World
Icg2001	Gentle World
Greyerbaby	Lonely Princess
MarcusL	ABC Poetry
Seemann	Voyage
Wintersixfour	War
Lisasolonynko	If Morning Never Comes Again
VerticalStripe	Seasons
Daniela Turcanu	Seasons
Click	Seasons
AcrylicArtist	Seasons
BBoomerinDenial	Ode To A Poet
Rahulthadani	The River's Journey
Ncgraphics	The Writer
Flying Pete	Questions
Aramemlucia	Questions
Quicksandala	Questions
mjas	Questions
jclk8888	God Speaks
jdurham	Bathing Suit
dierregi	Weathered Friends
hilarycl	Weathered Friends
Jamierodriguez37	Weathered Friends
DebuloPhoto	Weathered Friends
hotblack	Sun Rise

Your photographs provided me the opportunity to bring my poems to life.

LIVING LIFE IS LIKE

A STRAIGHT LINE – easy, not complicated – Until something happens to cause you to

A CURVE – you have to know when to bend at the right moment – Pray standing up, Pray while on bending knees

A CIRCLE – days when you go around and around – To create a Spiritual Connection with

A TRIANGLE – 3 points morning, noon and night –
The Father, The Son, and The Holy Spirit

A RECTANGLE or A SQUARE – boxed in on all 4 sides – So you can Pray in the mist of your Trials and Tribulations

Every Straight Line will become a Curve, a Circle, a Triangle, a Rectangle or a Square –
Each one teaches
SPIRITUAL WISDOW

RANDOM

THOUGHTS

Punctuation Marks and the Bible

Apostrophe – we belong to God

Brackets – we can never change God's words

Colon – invitation from God

Comma – additional information God wants us to know

Dash – God's words keep you on the right path

Ellipsis – we can never omit or erase who the Creator is

Exclamation Mark – Declare who God is and what He has done

Hyphen – does not apply when you have prayed

Parentheses – remove the things that don't fit into our spiritual relationship with God

Period – God's work and His every word is from everlasting to everlasting.

Quotation Mark – God said it, so shall it be

Semi-colon – when you pray, expect an answer

Slash – God gives us the choice to choose between good and evil

WHAT DOES YOUR SPIRITUAL REPORT CARD SAY?

AMEN because I am able to
BOW down at the feet of
CHRIST when I encounter the
DEVIL who puts my
FAITH on trail
I am glad to receive the FAITH because
without it, I cannot defeat the DEVIL
He is powerless against CHRIST
The one I BOW down to in prayer
To help me become victorious in my Spiritual Warfare AMEN

TODAY'S REMINDER –

You can't love others if you don't love yourself first. The love I speak of is Self-Respect and not Self-Pride, Self-Endurance and not Self-Unwillingness. If you Respect yourself you will know how to not allow your Pride to stand in the way of forcing a person to respect you. If you learn to tolerate much, you will be willing to go the distance with a person who can't go at it alone. Write yourself a Love Letter today and share it with another person.

HAVE YOU EVER –

Have you ever seen strength? YES - When I was weak I looked beyond myself

Have you ever talked with courage? YES - I spoke in silence and the voice within spoke truth

Have you ever faced determination? YES - I kept climbing until I reached the top of my failures

Have you ever met Faith? Yes - I started to believe when I prayed

Strength, courage, determination and faith has one name - ME.

It took all of these things for me to step outside of myself so I can look back at myself

JOY

SORROW

HOPE

PEACE

Photographer: jdurham

BOOK OF SECRETS

I remember when I was small
spending time at my grandmother's house
was a favorite time of mine

My grandmother was a great cook,
she was always in the kitchen,
standing at the stove, stirring the pot
and reading from her book

The cover of her book was black,
the edges trimmed in gold,
there was no title and it looked very old

Then one day I said to her "grandma
why do you always read that book every
time you cook?
Is that your Book of Secrets for all of your
recipes?"

She said "no it's not and I promise one day
it will be yours when I don't need it anymore"

As the years past by and I grew older,
she was still reading her book
All I could do was patiently wait,
hoping someday I could read it too

Then one day she passed away, oh, how I cried
I picked up her book from the kitchen table
and read the inscription inside

The inscription read
TO MY GRANDDAUGHTER
THE GRATEST GIFT I LEAVE FOR YOU
.....MY HOLY BIBLE

Photographer: jkt_de

SHIP OF LIFE

GOD is the MASTER
Of my FAITH
JESUS is the CAPTAIN
Of my SOUL
When I am sailing
On my Ship of Life
The storms don't last very long

My Ship of Life
Is beaten and worn
With GOD as my MASTER
And JESUS as my CAPTAIN
My Ship of Life keeps sailing on

The Storms of Life will forever
Rage on
With GOD watching from above
And JESUS onboard
My Ship of Life
Keeps sailing through troubled storms

When my Ship of Life reaches
That distant shore
All of my troubles will be left onboard
Because my Ship of Life
Will be anchored
In GOD'S MERCY
And blessed with JESUS' LOVE

Photograher: Prawny

Photographer: hotblack

Photograhper: hotblack

Photographer: Icg2001

GENTLE WORLD

If only we can hold on and love one another
Like the Lion and the Lamb, side by side
Allowing Love to be our guide

Let the Dove fly high in the sky
The same way it flew from Noah's Ark
Returning with an olive leaf to let us
Know the world is now at peace

Stop the hatred, the violence
And senseless killings
Let us unite together with love, respect
And the spirit of selfless giving

Harboring hatred and evil in our hearts,
This world will never be at peace
Oh, what a Gentle World so many of us long
For this world to be

Photographer: greyerbaby

LONELY PRINCESS

Oh, my sweet, sweet Prince, where forth are thou
I stand in the mist of darkness waiting for you
My days are dark and my nights are long
How much longer until you are
home and in my arms

Without you holding me in your arms
My yearning for your love leaves
my heart empty and alone
How much longer must my heart suffer?
Longing for your love in the darkness of night
Without your love, there is no sunlight

I feel as if I'm drowning in a sea of tears
If only I can hear your soft voice
whispering in my ears
The presence of your love will remove all my fears
My sweet, sweet Prince,
please return to me soon
So we can once again be together
Dancing under the stars and the moon

Photographer: MarcusL

ABC POETRY

A Bountiful Creation Dawning Early
From God's Heaven
In Joy, Kind, Love
Moving Naturally

Optimal Precious Quantum
Reflecting Sunshine
Thespian Uniformed Visions
Without Xanthippe,
Yesterdays Zephyr

Photographer: Seemann

VOYAGE

I started my voyage with no plan in mind
I just wanted to sail far away into another time
I kept on sailing until I was far from shore
To find peace and quiet, maybe, another world

Now I'm sailing out in a sea of darkness,
All alone on this forsaken voyage
I know not where my ship will go
To reach dry land, is my prayer and hope

Maybe this voyage is a reflection of my life,
Am I lost and alone with no hope in sight?
Surely my life is worth much more
The answer might be found on a distant shore

Until such time my ship alit, I'll keep sailing
On the dark sea of life
One day I will find that special place
To fill my heart with joy and happiness
Instead of this voyage of emptiness

Photographer: wintersixfour

WAR

(Countrymen, What Have You Done)

Can you see what you have done
to our daughters and sons

They went away to fight in your war
Some returned home displaying
behavioral problems; traumatized and lost

Can you see what you have done
to our daughters and sons

Others returned home with missing limbs
You gave them a prosthetic leg or arm
Then you say they are healed

How many more wars do they have to fight
before you can see the devastation and
destruction, the loss of so many lives

Can you see what you have done
to our daughters and sons?

WHAT'S

ON

MY

MIND

DISTANCE –

The distance you will go in life is unmeasured because you will take one step at a time. Whether your steps are in thoughts or deeds, the distance of your life is still unmeasured because your thoughts and your deeds are endless.

FOOD FOR THOUGHT –

When you trying to move forward and you feel as if you are moving backwards, just stand still. Standing still does not mean you are not moving, it only means you are where you are suppose to be for that moment in your life.

WALKING –

If I walk behind you it is not because I want you to lead, it's because I will catch you when you fall. If I walk in front of you it's not because I want to lead, it's because I am making your path clear of danger. If I am walking by your side, it's because you can lean on me when you need to....Tell this to another person and have them repeat it back to you. - The reaction of how a few words can create something amazing in your life.

ACKNOWLEDGE YOURSELF TODAY –

A good plan in life to be successful is a plan to strengthen your weakness to prevent failure. If you are not failing, you are succeeding. Grow in strength by acknowledging your weakness. You would be amazed at how successful you really are.

PLANT ME SOMETHING TO GROW –

Your life didn't start from where you are; it started from the seed that was planted, which became a root. If you damage or destroy the root, you will damage or destroy yourself. Nobody can thrive without a root. *I AM THE ROOT OF YOUR BEGINNING* so when you branch out in life, I am still rooted in you.

Photographer: lisasolonynko

IF THE MORNING NEVER COMES

If the morning never comes again for me,
would the world still exist!
I won't be here to see it,
No need for me to wonder if I will be missed

If the morning never comes again for me,
I will be alright because years before
The new morning dawned I tried to live a righteous life

If the morning never comes again for me,
all my troubles the day before
With the new morning dawning,
my troubles will be no more

If the morning never comes again for me,
one thing I know for sure
The yesteryears that I have lived
I lived a full life, morning, noon and night

If the morning never comes again for me,
this is what I want people to know
I was a child of GOD while living on this earth

If the morning never comes again for me,
it won't matter to me if I am missed
I was highly favored in GOD'S eye sight.
My spirit is care free, full of GOD'S Heavenly Bliss

If the morning never comes again for me,
I will suffer no more
Because the dawn of the new morning,
GOD allowed me entrance into
Heaven's door,
I will be with GOD, in my Heavenly home

SUMMER Photographer: *VerticalStripe*

Photographer: Daniela Turcanu *FALL*

WINTER Photographer: *Click*

AcrylicArtist *SPRING*

SEASONS

SUMMER is the season when the
Days are filled with sunshine
Vacations and fun things to do
Carefree, no sense of time

Summer goes away, here comes **FALL**
Orange colored skies,
The leaves on the trees
Begin to change colors
They fall, creating
A leafy blanket covering the ground

Fall is over here comes **WINTER**
The weather is cold
Frost on the ground
The fireplace is lit in
All the homes

Winter blows over
SPRING is on her way
Signs of new life blooming
At the beginning of each new day

Each season comes and goes at their appointed time
Their cycle is complete
Again, it is **SUMMER**
When we all relax and have fun

Photographer: BBoomerinDenial

ODE TO A POET

You are a Poet, indeed you are
The words you write
Resonates deep within so many hearts

The way you pen your words
Is masterfully crafted
Poetry in motion
Full of joy, sorrow, peace, hope
And laughter

Whether you write complete stanzas
Or only a few lines
You take your reader on the same journey
You created in your mind

You have talent and you are skilled
You are the poet
The world needs to hear

Photographer: rahulthadani

THE RIVER'S JOURNEY

Mighty are the Rivers
They flow from North to South
East to West
They all meet together
They never stop,
They never rest

Mighty are the Rivers
Constantly ever moving
No matter their direction
In which they flow

Without the Mighty Rivers
Life cannot continue
Nothing or no one can
Flourish or grow

Mighty are the Rivers
No man can control
The Rivers are their
Own source

Mighty are their strengths
The way they make things grow

Mighty are the Rivers
They were created by
Mother Nature

They meet together at
Their appointed time
Mother Nature controls
The Rivers, not mankind

Photographer: ncgraphics

THE WRITER

There is a *Book of Secrets* the Writer writes
the book is about all the things they do from
the time they are born to the day they die

Some write about discerning lifestyles,
which indicates a *Blanket of Darkness*,
masquerading the true nature of what they
might feel inside

Some write about the *Shades of Fall*
while sitting in their favorite chair
watching the *October Rain* drops
clean smog from the air

Some write lyrics for love songs
while looking up at the starlit sky
They find themselves humming the tune
creating a song titled
Romancing The Moon

Some write about *The Jewels of the Faeries*
creating a magical tale, to be read to children
when it's time for them to go to bed

Then, there are those who write about
A Gate of Dreams, taking the reader to a
*Gentle Place, Where the Angels Fly –
From Where The Fall – In Violet Lights*
to mend their broken wings

Every Writer has a story that needs to be told
The greatest reward *the Writer* receives is to know
Their story touched the reader's heart and soul

ABYSS of DARKNESS

Photographer: Flying Pete

SHADOWED REALM

Photographer: caramemlucia

SEVEN PLANETS

Photographe: quicksandala

PLAINS OF ETERNITY

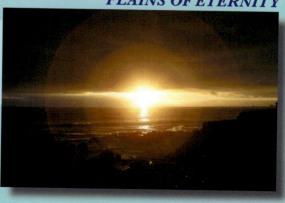

Photograpger: mjas

QUESTIONS

What is the Abyss of Darkness?
Does anybody really know?
Do you get there passing through
Two Dimensions into Space
Somewhere between Heaven and Earth

When the Spirit ascends into outer space
Before it reaches the Shadowed Realm
Possible Gateway to the Seventh Heaven
Is the Spirit in a holding pattern?
Called the First Limbo Stage

Does Heaven consist of Seven Planets?
Each with Empty Halls
Where we take a Spiritual Test
To determine the fate of the Spirit
Before it reaches the Inverted Ream of Oblivion
Where the Mysterious Band of Angels
Might be waiting?

When we die where will our spirit go?
Will it go to the Hall of Immortals?
Or, will it go to the Plains of Eternity?
God is the only one who knows the
Answers to all of the questions

THINKING

OUT

LOUD

JUST ME –

My heart was not healed by the broken things that were repaired. My heart was healed by the humbleness of my soul. A humble soul creates a peaceful spirit. The Peace of God rules in my heart. I am thankful.

LIFE SUCH AS IT IS,
Is a silent moment embedded in time
Make your life worth while living
The Good, The Bad, The Indifferent
Because when you are done living
SOMEBODY, will still remember YOUR LIFE, such as it was,
Will become a MEMORIAL
moment talked about for a LIFETIME

A TASTE OF GOODNESS –
When you opened your eyes this morning, no matter what you thought, GOD'S MERCY and GRACE was with you. Open your heart so your spirit can taste HIS GOODNESS.

PEOPLE –
Sometime when people try their best to avoid you it's not because you did something wrong, oftentimes, it's because you did something right and when this happens you know you made an impact on their life. Their negative way of thinking gave you an opportunity to allow the goodness in you to be a beacon of hope for them.

REJOICE

AND

SMILE

BOOK OF JOB

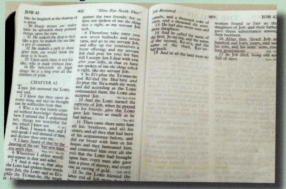

BOOK OF PSALMS

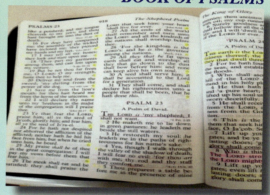

BOOK OF PROVERBS

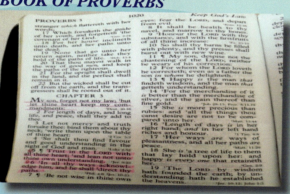

BOOK OF MATTHEW

Photographer of All Photos: R M Lampkin

WHAT SHOULD YOU DO

When you think life is too hard
You find yourself feeling lost and alone
Read the "Book of Job" He lost everything
His story gives you strength
The "WILL" to be strong

When you are confused
you don't know what to do
You can't find anybody to talk to
Read the "Book of Psalms"
The words will be a "GUIDE" for you

When you lack knowledge
and you don't understand
You are filled with doubt
Read the "Book of Proverbs"
Words full of "WISDOM" to help you out

When your soul is troubled
You don't need to worry
You don't need to fret
Read the "Book of Matthew"
And do what "JESUS" said

Photographer: jclk8888

GOD SPEAKS

(When I Repent)

Dry your eyes, please don't cry
I know the reasons why you cry
The words GOD spoke to me
When the first tear drops fell from my eyes

Many storms have come my way
Each time I sought shelter in YOU
During my trials and tribulations
YOU keep me safe

There are times when I am afraid
But I know I am not alone
YOU always send me a COMFORTER to
Give me strength and keep me strong

I will keep YOUR WORDS
in my heart forever more
So each time I cry, my COMFORTER
Will be there to quiet my spirit and
Give rest to my weary soul

Dry your eyes, please don't cry
I know the reasons why you cry
The words GOD spoke to me
Each and every time I've cried

Photographer: jdurham

BATHING SUIT

Summer is the season I look forward to
It's that time of year for me to wear my bathing suit
I skip work to go to the beach, tanning in the sun,
relaxed, care-free and having fun

Summer is over and here comes Fall
The weather is cool, nighttime comes early
The fog rolls in, here come the mist
I wear a sweater, long pants and shoes
instead of wearing my bathing suit

The next season coming I know oh so well
Here comes Ol' Man Winter, bringing with him
rain, sleet, snow and hail
Summer has passed; The Fall Season is gone
Time to put on the mittens, the heavy coat and boots
For sure, I can't wear my bathing suit

Winter blows over, say goodbye Ol' Man Winter
Spring is finally here
A time to dress in bright colors - orange,
yellow, green, red or blue

Soon, it will be Summer again
Oh darn, can I still fit into my bathing suit?

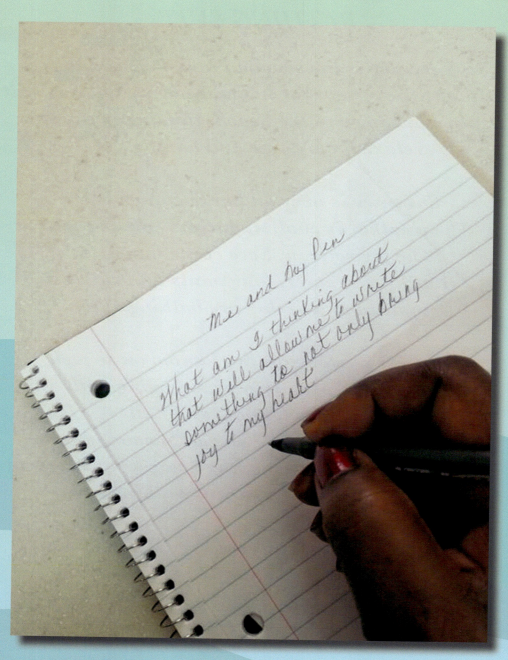

ME AND MY PEN

I am a writer
This is what I love to do
Writing brings me peace
A magical and mysterious sense
Giving me hope and strength

I write about joy, I write about sorrow
I write about hope and fear
Living life yesterday, today, and tomorrow
Better days into my golden years

No matter what I write about
Writing helps me release my inner spirit
Giving me a reason to allow my soul
To sing, rejoice and be thankful for the
Gift I have been given

RAIN

Photographer: dierregi

WIND

Photographer: hilarycl

HAIL, SLEET, and SNOW

Photographer: Jamierodriguez37

SUNSHINE

Photographer: DebuloPhoto

WEATHERED FRIENDS

I have one friend, she is like RAIN
She tells me all of her troubles,
Oh, too much information
She is flooding my brain

Another friend of mine
She reminds me of the WIND
As if she is riding the rapids
Moving too fast
Now, she chills my skin

Yes, another one
She is like HAIL, SLEET and SNOW
She slips and slides all day long
She can't understand why she
Struggles with success to grow

My friend who is like SUNSHINE
She always brighten my day
Thinking about her
Is a "much needed" breath of fresh air

They say I am the Care-free one,
It doesn't matter how we are,
Whenever we are together
We are simple, we have fun

Photographer: hotblack

SUN RISE

Looking at the Sun Rise
What do you see?
I see a Glorious Creation
Looking back at me

I am so amazed of
Its morning light
The amount of Joy
The Sun Rise brings to
My Life

I look forward to see another
Sun Rise
So I can be Thankful
For another day in
My Life

Enjoy the Sun Rise
It is GOD'S Glorious Light

Printed in the United States
By Bookmasters